D0769331

My First Animal Library

Brown Bears

by Cari Meister

Bullfrog Books

Ideas for Parents and Teachers

Bullfrog Books let children practice reading informational text at the earliest reading levels. Repetition, familiar words, and photo labels support early readers.

Before Reading

- Discuss the cover photo. What does it tell them?

- Look at the picture glossary together. Read and discuss the words.

Read the Book

- "Walk" through the book and look at the photos. Let the child ask questions. Point out the photo labels.

- Read the book to the child, or have him or her read independently.

After Reading

- Prompt the child to think more. Ask: How are mother bears like your parents? What would you do if you saw a bear with her cubs?

Bullfrog Books are published by Jump!
5357 Penn Avenue South
Minneapolis, MN 55419
www.jumplibrary.com

Library of Congress Cataloging-in-Publication Data

Meister, Cari, author.
  Brown bears / by Cari Meister.
     pages cm. — (Bullfrog books. My first animal library)
  Audience: Age 5.
  Audience: K to grade 3.
  Includes index.
  ISBN 978-1-62031-166-0 (hardcover) —
  ISBN 978-1-62496-253-0 (ebook)
  1. Brown bear — Juvenile literature. I. Title.
  QL737.C27M453 2015
  599.784—dc23
                                        2014032119

Series Editor: Wendy Dieker
Series Designer: Ellen Huber
Book Designer: Anna Peterson
Photo Researcher: Casie Cook

Photo Credits: All photos by Shutterstock except: Corbis, 8; Getty: 6–7, 18–19, 23br; National Geographic: 16–17; NPL: 10–11; SuperStock: 14–15, 20–21; Thinkstock: cover, 17, 24.

Printed in the United States of America at Corporate Graphics in North Mankato, Minnesota.

Table of Contents

A Winter Sleeper

It's winter.

A brown bear sleeps.
She is hibernating.

A cub grows in her belly.
Soon, he is born.
He is tiny.

cub

He crawls up
his mama's fur.

He drinks
her milk.

He grows and grows.

Spring is here.

Mama is hungry!

The bears leave the den.

den

Mama stands on two legs.
Now she can see better.

She sniffs.
She smells fish
in the river!

The bears walk to the river.

Cubs get a ride.

Other bears are here.

One growls at the cub.

Mama shows her teeth.

The bear runs away.

Salmon jump.

Mama swats with her paw.

She grabs with her teeth.

salmon

She gets a fish.
Yum!

Parts of a Brown Bear

fur
Thick fur helps keep brown bears warm.

nose
Brown bears have a great sense of smell. They can smell things that are 15 miles (24 km) away.

teeth
Brown bears have long, sharp canines.

claws
Brown bears use their curved claws to dig dens and to rip open their food.

Picture Glossary

cub
A baby bear.

hibernate
When an animal spends the winter sleeping or resting.

den
A cave or hole where a brown bear makes a home.

salmon
A large fish that is born in a stream or river.

Index

To Learn More

Learning more is as easy as 1, 2, 3.

1) Go to www.factsurfer.com

2) Enter "brown bears" into the search box.

3) Click the "Surf" button to see a list of websites.

With factsurfer.com, finding more information is just a click away.